CW01424459

Knights of Malta

1523–1798

THE LOTHIAN PRIZE ESSSAY FOR 1920

Knights of Malta

1523–1798

R. Cohen

ÆGYPAN PRESS

1920

Knights of Malta, 1523–1798
A publication of
ÆGYPAN PRESS
www.aegypan.com

Table of Contents

Chapter I

SETTLEMENT AT MALTA, 1523–1565

On January 1, 1523, a fleet of fifty vessels put out from the harbor at Rhodes for an unknown destination in the West. On board were the shattered remnants of the Order of St. John of Jerusalem, accompanied by 4,000 Rhodians, who preferred the Knights and destitution to security under the rule of the Sultan Solyman. The little fleet was in a sad and piteous condition. Many of those on board were wounded;

all — Knights and Rhodians alike — were in a state of extreme poverty. For six months they had resisted the full might of the Ottoman Empire under its greatest Sultan, Solyman the Magnificent; Europe had looked on in amazed admiration, but had not ventured to move to its rescue. Now they were leaving the home their Order had possessed for 212 years, and were sailing out to beg from Christendom another station from which to attack the infidel once again.

The Knights of Rhodes — as they were called at the time — were the only real survivors of the militant Order of Chivalry. Two centuries earlier their great rivals, the Templars, had been dissolved, and a large part of their endowments handed over to the Hospitallers. The great secret of the long and enduring success of the Order of St. John was their capacity for adapting themselves to the changing needs of the times. The final expulsion of the Christians from Syria had left the Templars idle and helpless, and the loss of the outlets for their energy soon brought corruption and decay with the swift consequence of dissolution. All through the history of the great Orders we find the Kings of Europe on the lookout for a chance to seize their possessions: any excuse or pretext is used, sometimes most shamelessly. An Order of Knighthood that failed to perform the duties for which it was founded was soon overtaken by disaster.

The Hospitallers had realized, as early as 1300, that their former rôle of mounted Knights fighting on land was gone forever. From their seizure of Rhodes, in 1310, they became predominantly seamen, whose flag, with its eight-pointed cross, struck terror into every infidel heart. Nothing but a combination of Christian monarchs could cope with the superiority of the Turk on land: by sea he was still vulnerable. The Knights took up their new part with all their old energy and determination: it is but typical that henceforward we never hear of the "Knights" of Malta fighting as cavalry.

After various adventures the fleet found itself united at Messina, whence it proceeded to Baiae. The election to the papacy of the Cardinal de' Medici — one of their own Order — as Clement VII, gave the Knights a powerful protector. He assigned Viterbo as a residence for the Order till a permanent home had been discovered.

Villiers de L'Isle Adam, Grand Master of the Order, was faced with many difficulties. Remembering the fate of the Templars, he was afraid that the Order would disperse, and its present helpless condition was surely tending to disintegration. At this time the war between Charles V and Francis I was at its height, and the quarrel between France and Spain was reflected within the ranks of the Hospitallers. As the French and Spanish Knights formed the greater part of the members, the unity of the Order was threatened by the quarrels between them that arose out of national sentiment. The Reformation was rapidly spreading, and was likely to prove dangerous to the lands of the

Order in Northern Europe, and various monarchs were meditating the seizure of the Hospitallers' estates now that the Order was temporarily without a justification for its existence.

The Grand Master showed himself a skillful diplomat, as well as a brave soldier. From 1523 to 1530 the Order remained without a home, while L'Isle Adam visited the different European courts to stay the grasping hands of the various Kings. All this time negotiations were proceeding between Charles V and the Knights for the cession of Malta. The harsh conditions which the Emperor insisted upon in his offer made the Knights reluctant to accept, while his preoccupation with the war against France made negotiations difficult. Further, the cause of the Knights had been damaged when the Pope — who had acted as their intercessor — joined the ranks of Charles's enemies, and Clement VII was now a prisoner in the Emperor's hands. In March, 1530, an agreement was finally arrived at, which was the most favorable the Emperor would grant. One harassing burden the Knights could not escape: Charles insisted that Tripoli must go with Malta, a gift which meant a useless drain upon their weak resources, and which fell in 1551 to Dragut-Reis and the Turkish forces at the first serious attack. L'Isle Adam had insisted that he could not take the island over as a feudatory to the King of Spain, as that was contrary to the fundamental idea of the Order — its impartiality in its relations to all the Christian Powers. The only condition of service, therefore, that was made was nominal: the Grand Master henceforth was to send, on All Souls' Day, a falcon to the Viceroy of Sicily as a token of feudal sub-mission.*

This was a splendid bargain for the Emperor. Malta had hitherto been worthless to him, but henceforth it became one of the finest bulwarks of his dominions. To understand the supreme value of the island, we must take a glance at sea power in the Mediterranean in the sixteenth century.

---

* *Vide* Appendix I.

The beginning of the century had seen the growth of the Corsairs' strength to a most alarming extent. While all the European Powers were fighting among themselves, these Barbary Corsairs (as they were later called) had become the terror of the Western Mediterranean. Spain, by its unrelenting persecution of the Moriscoes, following on centuries of bitter conflict between Christian and Mussulman, had earned the undying hatred of the dwellers on the North African coast, many of whom were the children of the expelled Moors. These Moors had wasted their energy in desultory warfare up to the beginning of the sixteenth century, when the genius of the two brothers, Uruj and Khair-ed-Din Barbarossa, had organized them into the pirate State of Algiers, which was to be a thorn in the side of Christendom for over three centuries. The Corsairs were not content with merely attacking ships at sea: they made raids on the Spanish, Italian, and Sicilian sea-boards, burning and looting for many miles inland. The inhabitants of these parts were driven off as captives to fill the bagnios of Algiers, Tunis, Bizerta, and other North African towns. These prisoners were used as galley slaves, and the life of a galley slave was generally so short that there was no difficulty of disposing of all the captives that could be seized. Cupidity, allied with fanaticism, gave this state of war a cruelty beyond conception: both sides displayed such undaunted courage and such fierce personal hatred as to make men wonder, even in that hard and bitter century. Those low-lying galleys, which were independent of the wind, were ideal pirates' craft in the gentle Mediterranean summer, and many a slumbering Spanish or Italian village would be startled into terror by their sudden approach. The audacity of their methods is illustrated by the raid on Fundi in 1534, when Barbarossa swooped down on that town simply to seize Giulia Gonzaga — reputed the loveliest woman in Italy — for the Sultan's harem: the fair Duchess of Trajetto hardly escaped in her nightdress.

The Eastern Mediterranean, after the capture of Rhodes, was almost entirely a Turkish preserve. Though Venice at this period still kept her hold on Cyprus and Crete, the former of which was not yielded by the Republic till 1573 and the latter till 1669, yet the Treaty of Constantinople in 1479 had definitely reduced the position of Venice in the Levant from an independent Power to a tolerated ally. The growth of the Ottoman sea power had been alarming enough, but it became a distinct menace to the Christian Powers of the Mediterranean when the Corsair chiefs of the North African coast became Turkish vassals. All the African coast from Morocco to Suez, the coast of Asia Minor, and the European coast from the Bosphorus to Albania (with the exception of a few islands), were in Turkish hands. From 1475, with the conquest of the Crimea, the Black Sea had become a Turkish lake, and under Solyman the Magnificent the Turks had become masters of Aden and the Red Sea, with a strong influence along the Arabian and Persian coasts.

Malta, then as always, was of supreme strategic importance for the domination of the Mediterranean. It lay right in the center of the narrow channel connecting the Eastern and Western Mediterranean, and, in the hands of such a small but splendidly efficient band of sailors as the Knights Hospitallers, was sure to become a source of vexation to the mighty Turkish Empire. Though not so convenient as Rhodes for attacking Turkish merchant shipping, yet it had one advantage, in that it lay close to Christian shores and could easily be succored in the hour of need. A small, highly defensible island, strengthened by all the resources of engineering, it could, and did, become one of the most invulnerable fortresses in the world, and of the utmost importance for the control of the Mediterranean.

Charles V, therefore, made a splendid bargain when he handed over the neglected island to the Order of St. John, even had the gift been unconditional. The Knights rendered him valuable service by sharing in the several expeditions the Spaniards undertook to the African coast. Barbarossa, by the capture of Tunis from the old Hafside dynasty in 1534, threatened the important channel between Sicily and Africa, which it was essential for Charles V to keep open. In the next year, therefore, the Emperor attacked the town and conquered it without much difficulty. The victory was unfortunately stained by the inhuman excesses of the Imperial troops, and Charles's hold on Tunis was very short-lived. In 1541 came the miserable fiasco of the Spanish expedition to Algiers. Here, also, the Knights behaved with their usual bravery; but Charles's disregard of the advice of his Admiral, Andrea Doria, resulted in the failure of the whole expedition. In these and other expeditions the Knights took part: some — like the attack in 1550 on Mehedia* — were successful, others — like the siege of the Isle of Jerbah in 1559 — ended in disaster.

---

* The chroniclers, such as Vertot, often call this town, which was the ancient Adrumetum, "Africa," and it is therefore necessary to watch their use of that word carefully.

Such was the importance of Malta when the Knights took over the island in 1530. The first need was to put it into a state of defense. On the northeast of the island was the promontory of Mount Sceberras, flanked by the two fine harbors, the Marsa Muscetto and what was later known as the Grand Harbor.* The eastern side of the Grand Harbor was broken by three prominent peninsulas, later occupied by Fort Ricasoli, Fort St. Angelo, and Fort St. Michael. The only fortification in 1530 was the Fort of St. Angelo, with a few guns and very weak walls. The intention of the Knights, even from the beginning, was to make the main peninsula, Mount Sceberras, the seat of their "Convent"; but as that would mean the leveling of the whole promontory, a task of enormous expense and difficulty, and as immediate defense was necessary, they decided to occupy the Peninsula of St. Angelo for the present. Wedged between St. Angelo and the mainland there was a small town, "Il Borgo": this, for the present, the

---

* See map on p. 30.

Knights made their headquarters, drawing a line of entrenchments across the neck of the promontory to guard it from the neighboring heights.

When it became certain that Malta was to be its permanent home — for L'Isle Adam had at first cherished hopes of recapturing Rhodes — the Order proceeded to take further measures for its security. Both St. Angelo and Il Borgo were strengthened with ramparts and artillery, and the fortifications of the Città Notabile, the main town in the center of the island, were improved. In 1552 a commission of three Knights with Leo Strozzi, the Prior of Capua, at its head — one of the most daring Corsairs of the day — made a report of the fortifications of the island. They recommended strengthening Il Borgo and St. Angelo, and pointed out that the whole promontory was commanded by St. Julian, the southernmost of the three projections into the Grand Harbor. Further, as it was necessary to command the entrances both of Marsa Muscetto and of the Grand Harbor, the tip, at least, of Mount Sceberras should be occupied, as the finances of the Order would not allow of anything further being done. These recommendations were carried out, and Fort St. Michael was built on St. Julian and Fort St. Elmo on the end of Mount Sceberras. A few years later the Grand Master de la Sangle supplied the obvious deficiencies of St. Julian by enclosing it on the west and the south by a bastioned rampart.

Now the commitments of the Order in Tripoli proved a constant drain on its resources. Time after time Charles V was appealed to for help in holding Tripoli, which was very difficult to fortify because of the sandy nature of the soil, and difficult to succor because of its distance from Malta. But Charles V was at once reluctant to let go his grip of any parts of the African coast, and too much absorbed by his own troubles to be able to render much help, however much he might have desired to do so. It was obvious that the first determined attack of the Turks would mean the fall of Tripoli. In 1551, after putting in an appearance off Malta,

Dragut, the successor of Barbarossa, sailed to Tripoli and easily captured the place owing to the disaffection of the mercenary troops in the garrison.

During this period, 1523–1565, the Order lost forever one of the eight national divisions or "langues." Henry VIII, soon after the fall of Rhodes, had shown himself unfriendly to the interests of the Order, but had been appeased by a visit of L'Isle Adam in February, 1528.* But Henry's proceedings against the Pope and the monasteries inevitably involved the Order of St. John, which had large possessions both in England and in Ireland. The Grand Priory of England was situated at Clerkenwell, and the Grand Prior held the position in the House of Lords of the connecting link between the Lords Spiritual and the Barons, coming after the former in rank and before the latter. There is extant a letter written by Henry VIII in 1538 to the Grand Master, Juan

* This visit caused a great sensation in Europe, as De L'Isle Adam crossed the Alps in the depth of winter, and this haste to pay his respects touched the King of England.

d'Omedes, wherein conditions are laid down for the maintenance of the Order in England. The two main stipulations were, that any Englishman admitted into the Order must take an oath of allegiance to the King, and that no member in England must in any way recognize the jurisdiction or authority of the Pope. Henry was well aware that the Knights could never consent to terms such as these, which were the negation of the fundamental principle of international neutrality of their Order. Henry's offers were refused, and the English langue, which had a brilliant record in the Order, perished. Many of the Knights fled to Malta; others were executed for refusing obedience to the Act of Supremacy. A general confiscation of their property took place, and in April, 1540, an Act of Parliament was passed vesting all the property of the Order in the Crown, and setting aside from the revenues of such properties certain pensions to be paid to the Lord Prior and other members. The Grand Prior, Sir William

Weston, died soon after, before he could enjoy his pension of £1,000 a year.

With the accession of Mary, in 1553, negotiations were at once opened with the Knights for the restoration of the English langue, and during her reign the old Order was restored once again, though the lands were not returned. But Elizabeth, in the first year of her reign, suppressed the Knights for good and all.

In North Africa, Philip II, on his accession, had taken over the troubles of his father, and after the Corsairs had failed in their attack on the Spanish ports of Oran and Mazarquivir, he carried the war once more into the enemy's territory. Finding themselves isolated, they appealed to their overlord, the aged Sultan Solyman, to help them against Spain.

The most important seaman on the Turkish side was Dragut — Pasha of Tripoli since 1551 — who had been the greatest of Barbarossa's lieutenants. In 1540 Dragut had been surprised and captured by Giannetin Doria, the nephew of the great Admiral, and had served four years chained to the bench of a Genoese galley. One of the last acts of Khair-ed-Din Barbarossa had been to ransom his follower in the port of Genoa, in 1544, for 3,000 crowns, an arrangement of which the Genoese afterwards sorely repented. Dragut had the ear of the Sultan when the appeal for help came from Africa, and his suggestion was to attempt the capture of Malta. It had become more and more certain that the Turks would not leave the island unassailed. Not only did the Knights lend splendid help to the various Christian Powers, but they were in themselves a formidable foe. Their fleet was always small, six or seven galleys, but they became the dread of every Turkish vessel in the Mediterranean. Annually these red galleys, headed by their black *capitana,* swooped down on the Turkish shipping of the Levant and brought back many rich prizes. Malta grew steadily in wealth, and the island became full of Turkish slaves. The generals of the Maltese galleys, Strozzi, La Valette, Charles of Lorraine, and De Romegas, were far more terrible even than the great Corsairs, because of their determination to extirpate the infidel. The state of war between the Order and the Mussulman was recognized by all as something unique; neither side dreamt of a peace or a truce, and only once in the history of the Order does there seem to have been the suggestion of an agreement. The fanaticism which actuated the Knights in their determination to destroy the infidel made them formidable enemies, despite their fewness in number. Solyman the Magnificent must have often repented of his clemency in letting the Knights leave Rhodes alive, and in 1564 he decided it would be a fitting end to his reign if he could destroy the worst pest of the Mediterranean by capturing Malta and annihilating the Order of St. John of Jerusalem.

Chapter II

THE SIEGE OF MALTA, 1565

The Grand Master of the Knights of Malta in 1565 was Jean Parisot de la Valette. Born in 1494 of a noble family in Quercy, he had been a Knight of St. John all his life, and forty-three years before had distinguished himself at the siege of Rhodes. He had never left his post at the "Convent" except to go on his "caravans,"* as the cruises in the galleys were named. As a commander of the galleys of the "Religion," as

* A reminiscence of the Syrian days of the Order.

the Order called itself, he had won a name that stood conspicuous in that age of great sea captains; and in 1557, on the death of the Grand Master de la Sangle, the Knights, mindful of the attack that was sure to come, elected La Valette to the vacant office. No better man could be found even in the ranks of the Order. Passionately religious, devoted body and soul to his Order and faith, Jean de la Valette was prepared to suffer all to the death rather than yield a foot to the hated infidel. Unsparing of himself, he demanded utter sacrifice from his subordinates, and his cold, unflinching severity would brook no hesitation.

Both sides spent the winter and spring of 1565 in preparations for the great attack. The Grand Master sent a message to all the Powers of Europe; but Philip II, who sent him some troops, and the Pope, who sent him 10,000 crowns, alone responded to his appeal. The message sent to the various commanderies*

---

* The name given to the different estates of the Hospitallers scattered throughout Europe: they were so called because they were each in charge of a "commander," sometimes also

throughout Europe brought the Knights in haste to the defense of their beloved Convent. The Maltese Militia was organized and drilled and proved of great value in the siege, and even 500 galley slaves were released on promise of faithful service. Altogether La Valette seems to have had at his disposal about 9,000 men (though the authorities differ slightly as to the exact figures). Of these over 600 were Knights with their attendants, about 1,200 were hired troops, about 1,000 were volunteers, chiefly from Italy, and the remainder Maltese Militia and galley slaves.

The Turkish fleet at the beginning consisted of 180 vessels, of which 130 were galleys; and the troops on board consisted of about 30,000 men, of whom 6,000 belonged to the select troops of the Janissaries. Twice during the siege the Ottomans received reinforcements: first, Dragut himself with 13 galleys and 1,600 men, and later, Hassan, Viceroy of Algiers and

---

named a "preceptor," from his duty of receiving and training novices.

son of Khair-ed-Din Barbarossa, with 2,500 Corsairs. Altogether the Ottoman forces at the maximum, inclusive of sailors, must have exceeded 40,000 men. A small reinforcement of 700 men, of whom 42 were Knights, contrived to steal through the Turkish lines on June 29; but that was all the help the garrison received before September.

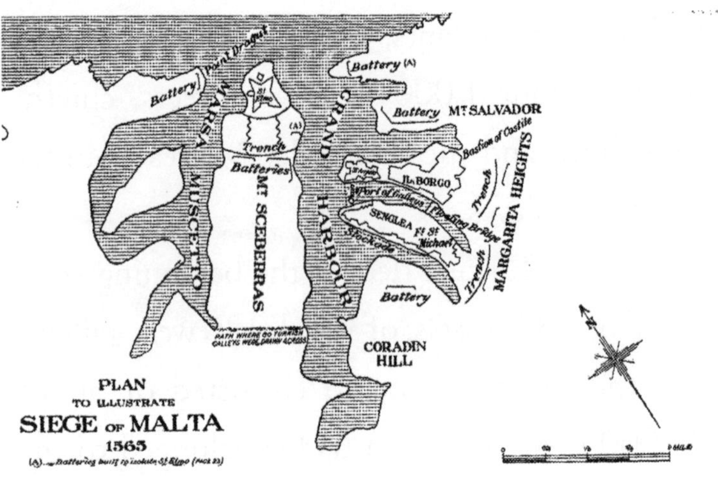

The Turkish army was under the command of Mustapha Pasha, and the fleet under that of Piali. Both had received orders not to take any steps without the advice of Dragut. It would have been far better for the Turkish cause had the Corsair been in supreme command, for his skill as an artilleryman was famous. But there had always been trouble in the Ottoman fleet when a Corsair was in command. The proud Turkish generals were unwilling to be under the orders of men who were of doubtful antecedents, and whom they despised in their hearts as low-born robbers. Even Barbarossa, acknowledged by all to be the greatest seaman in the Turkish Empire, could not enforce strict obedience in the campaign of Prevesa in 1538. The Grand Vizier Ibrahim had seen the folly of putting generals in command of fleets, and had therefore secured the promotion of Barbarossa: but Ibrahim was now dead, and Solyman, bereft of his wise counsel, made a compromise.

On May 18 the Turkish fleet was sighted off the island, and almost immediately the army disembarked, partly at Marsa Scirocco, and partly at St. Thomas's Bay. The first misfortune was the non-appearance of Dragut at the rendezvous, and in his absence Mustapha and Piali decided to attack St. Elmo and to leave to Dragut the responsibility of sanctioning the operations or breaking them off. Batteries were erected on Mount Sceberras, in which ten 80-pounders were brought into action, besides a huge basilisk throwing balls of 160 pounds, and two 60-pounder *coulevrines.* The Turks at the height of their power put great faith in novel and massive artillery, which, though clumsy, and at times more dangerous to their own gunners than the enemy, was terribly effective at the short distance it was placed from St. Elmo. The walls of the fortress soon began to crumble under the continuous bombardment, and the garrison, which had been increased to 120 Knights and two companies of Spanish infantry, soon felt the position untenable without reinforcements. As an attack had not yet been delivered La Valette was incensed at the appeal for help and offered to go himself to hold the fort; his council dissuaded him from doing so, and he permitted 50 Knights and 200 Spanish troops to cross to St. Elmo. It was of the utmost importance that St. Elmo should be held to the last minute. Not only did it delay the attack on the main forts, but Don Garcia de Toledo, the Viceroy of Sicily, had made it a condition in his arrangements with the Grand Master, before the siege, that St. Elmo must be held if the reinforcements from Sicily were to be sent.

At this point—June 2—Dragut arrived with his galleys and expressed nothing but disapproval for the Turkish operations. He pointed out that the besiegers should have isolated the fortifications from the rest of the island before proceeding to attack St. Elmo; but, as the siege had started, he insisted on continuing it as vigorously as possible. He erected a powerful battery on the summit of Mount Sceberras, which swept both Fort St. Angelo and Fort St. Elmo, and erected another on the headland opposite St. Elmo on the other side of the Marsa Muscetto, which was henceforth known as Point Dragut.

As soon as this was done the bombardment restarted with relentless fury. The Knights made a sortie to destroy some of the Turkish guns, but were driven back, and the Turks then captured and held a covered way leading up to a ravelin; a few days later, taking advantage of the negligence of the garrison, they surprised the ravelin itself, and, but for the efforts of a Spanish officer, would have captured the fort. After desperate fighting the Knights were still holding the fort, but had been unable to recapture the ravelin. The next day another attack was made by Mustapha, but without avail; the ravelin remained in Turkish hands, but it had cost them 2,000 men.

It was a great gain, however; two guns were mounted on it, and all the Turkish artillery, including that of the galleys, began to play on the hapless fort. It was no question of a breach; the walls were gradually destroyed till there was nothing left of the enceinte but a mass of ruins. Every part of the fort was directly exposed to the fire of the two guns on the ravelin, and this exposure made the strain on the Knights intolerable.

The garrison sent a Knight, renowned for his bravery, to report these conditions to the Grand Master and to ask for permission to withdraw. La Valette, feeling it imperative that the fort should hold out to the last minute, sent him back with orders that it was to be defended to the end. The garrison, amazed by his reply, sent a prayer for relief, failing which they would sally forth, sword in hand, to meet their death in open fight rather than be buried like dogs beneath the ruins. The Grand Master received the request with the stern comment that, not only were their lives at the disposal of the Order, but the time and manner of their death; but to make sure that their complaints were justified he would send three Knights to investigate the condition of the fort. One of the three (probably in collusion with La Valette) maintained the fort could be held, and offered himself to hold it with volunteers, who were immediately forthcoming in large numbers; but when the message arrived at St. Elmo announcing that the garrison was to be relieved, there was consternation among the defenders, who, now realizing the ignominy of their prayer, sent out yet another request to St. Angelo, this time to be allowed to hold St. Elmo to the death. After some delay the Grand Master granted the permission.

This was June 14; on the 16th the Ottomans delivered a grand assault. The fort was attacked on three sides, from Mount Sceberras and on each flank. The guns of St. Angelo rendered great service all day by raking the attacking forces in enfilade, and especially by breaking up the flank attack from the side of the Grand Harbor. All day long the battle went on with unabating fury; time after time the Janissaries burst over the ruined walls, and each time they were repulsed. Attacked on all sides, the few defenders fought with dauntless heroism, and when the night fell the Maltese Cross still waved over the fort.

Reinforcements were dispatched as soon as night set in, and the volunteers far exceeded all requirements.

Now at last the Turkish commanders perceived that, to capture St. Elmo, it must be isolated from St. Angelo. In the course of the next few days a battery was constructed on the promontory at the entrance of the Grand Harbor where Fort Ricasoli stood in later times, and another was mounted on the side of Mount Sceberras to sweep the landing place beneath the fort. Both batteries cost many Turkish lives, but their construction and the extension of the investing trenches to the Grand Harbor meant the complete isolation of St. Elmo. The Turks sustained their greatest loss when Dragut, while superintending the works, received a wound from which a week later he died.

For three days twenty-six guns kept up the bombardment, and on the early morning of June 22 another grand assault was made. Three times repulsed and three times renewed, the attack failed in the end, and the handful of surviving Knights was left at nightfall in possession of their ruins. All attempts during the night to send reinforcements failed under the fire of Dragut's new batteries, and La Valette saw that his men were beyond all hope of rescue.

The sixty shattered survivors prepared for death; worn out, they betook themselves at midnight to their little chapel, where they confessed and received the Eucharist for the last time. Dawn found them waiting, even to the wounded, who had been placed in chairs sword in hand to receive the last onslaught. Incredible as it may appear, the first assault was driven back, but the attack finally broke up the defense, and, with the exception of a few Maltese who escaped by swimming, the garrison perished to a man.

June 24, St. John the Baptist's Day, was one of sorrow inside the beleaguered fortress. The Turks had soiled their victory by mutilating their dead foes and throwing them into the Grand Harbor; La Valette took reprisals, and from that time neither side thought of quarter.

Nor were the besiegers greatly elated; the tiny Fort of St. Elmo had delayed them for five weeks and had cost them 8,000 men and their best general. The Order had lost 1,300 men, of whom 130 were Knights, and the disparity of the losses shows the impatience and recklessness of the Turkish attacks.

Mustapha now transferred the main part of his army to the other side of the Grand Harbor, and, drawing a line of entrenchments along the heights on its eastern side, succeeded in investing completely the two peninsulas of Senglea and Il Borgo. Batteries were established and a constant bombardment commenced, the main target being Fort St. Michael at the end of Senglea, on which a converging fire was brought to bear. Unable to bring his fleet into the Grand Harbor under the guns of St. Angelo, Mustapha had eighty galleys dragged across the neck of Mount Sceberras and launched on the upper waters of the Grand Harbor. This was a blow to the besieged, as it meant an attack by sea as well as by land, and La Valette made all the preparations possible to meet the danger. Along the southwest side of Senglea, where the beach is low, he constructed, with the aid of his

Maltese divers, a very firm and powerful stockade to prevent the enemy galleys from running ashore, and he also linked up Il Borgo and Senglea with a floating bridge.

On July 15 the Turks delivered a grand assault by sea and by land. The attack by sea, under the command of the renegade Candellissa, proved the more formidable. At the critical moment the defenders were thrown into confusion by an explosion on the ramparts, during which the Turks were able to make their way through the stockade and into the fortress, being checked with difficulty by the desperate resistance of the garrison and finally driven out by a timely reinforcement sent by La Valette. Ten boatloads of troops sent by Mustapha incautiously exposed themselves to the guns of St. Angelo and were almost all sunk, while the attack on the land side, led by Hassan, Viceroy of Algiers and son of Khaired-Din Barbarossa, proved an utter failure.

As at the siege of Rhodes, so at Malta, a distinct part of the fortifications had been allotted to each langue to defend. The langue of Castile held the northeast section of Il Borgo, which was destined to be the scene of most desperate fighting.

On August 7 a joint attack was made on the land side of Senglea and on the bastion of Castile. On that day the Turks came nearer success than ever before or after. Mustapha's desperate attacks on Senglea were at last successful: masters of the breach made by their guns, the assailants' weight of numbers began to tell, and slowly the defenders were being pushed back inside the fortress. At this moment, to everyone's amazement, Mustapha sounded the retreat. The little garrison of the Città Notabile, which had been left alone by the Turks, had been raiding the enemy's lines as usual, and, hearing the grand assault was in progress, had made a determined attack on the Turkish entrenchments from behind, burning and slaying all they could find. The confusion arising from this started the rumor that Sicilian reinforcements had landed and were attacking the Turkish army.

Mustapha, in fear of being surrounded, drew off his troops in the moment of victory.

Meanwhile,* farther north, the Bastion of Castile had been almost captured by Piali. The rock at that part of the fortification was extremely hard, and the possibility of mines had occurred to none of the garrison. Piali, however, with great labor, had dug a mine which had been sprung that morning and had blown a huge gap in the ramparts. This unexpected attack threw the whole of Il Borgo into confusion, and, but for the Grand Master's promptitude and coolness of mind, the enemy had been masters of the fortress. Seizing a pike, La Valette rushed into the fight, and, inspired by his example, the Knights succeeded in driving the enemy out of the breach. He ordered the garrison to remain there all night, as he expected an attack under the cover of darkness, and insisted on taking the command himself. His subordinates protested

* Most historians make this event part of the attack of August 18. But Prescott (*Philip II*, vol. ii., p. 428) points out that Balbi, who is undoubtedly the best authority for the siege as he was one of the garrison, places it on August 7.

against this reckless exposure of a valuable life, but his precautions were justified when a Turkish attack made in the darkness was defeated by his prompt resistance.

The bombardment continued unceasingly, and on August 18 another desperate assault was made, which, like the other, failed. Yet the position of the besieged was becoming desperate: dwindling daily in numbers, they were becoming too feeble to hold the long line of fortifications; but, when his council suggested the abandonment of Il Borgo and Senglea and withdrawal to St. Angelo, La Valette remained obdurate.

Why the Viceroy of Sicily had not brought help will always remain a mystery. Possibly the orders of his master, Philip II of Spain, were so obscurely worded as to put on his own shoulders the burden of a decision; a responsibility which he was unwilling to discharge because the slightest defeat would mean exposing Sicily to the Turk. He had left his own son with La Valette, so he could hardly be indifferent to the fate of the fortress, and Malta in Turkish hands would soon have proved a curse to Sicily and Naples. Whatever may have been the cause of his delay, the Viceroy hesitated till the indignation of his own officers forced him to move, and then the battle had almost been won by the unaided efforts of the Knights. On August 23 came yet another grand assault, the last serious effort, as it proved, of the besiegers; it was thrown back with the greatest difficulty, even the wounded taking part in the defense. The plight of the Turkish forces, however, was now desperate. With the exception of St. Elmo, the fortifications were still intact. By working night and day the garrison had repaired the breaches, and the capture of Malta seemed more and more impossible. Those terrible summer months with the burning sirocco had laid many of the troops low with sickness in their crowded quarters; ammunition and food were beginning to run short, and the troops were becoming more and more dispirited at the failure of their numerous attacks and the unending toll of lives.

The death of Dragut, on June 23, had proved an incalculable loss, and the jealousy between Mustapha and Piali prevented their co-operation. The whole course of the siege had been marked by a feverish haste and a fear of interruption, which showed itself in ill-drawn plans. Dragut himself, early in the siege, had pointed out the necessity of more foresight, but his warnings went unheeded. The Turkish commanders took few precautions, and, though they had a huge fleet, they never used it with any effect except on one solitary occasion. They neglected their communications with the African coast and made no attempt to watch and intercept Sicilian reinforcements.

On September I Mustapha made his last effort, but all his threats and cajoleries had but little effect on his dispirited troops, who refused any longer to believe in the possibility of capturing those terrible fortresses. The feebleness of the attack was a great encouragement to the besieged, who now began to see hopes of deliverance. Mustapha's perplexity and indecision were cut short by the news of the arrival of Sicilian reinforcements in Melleha Bay. Hastily evacuating his trenches, he embarked his army; but, on learning that the new troops numbered but some 8,000, was overcome by shame and put ashore to fight the reinforcements. It was all in vain, however, for his troops would not stand the fierce charge of the newcomers, and, helped by the determination of his rearguard, safely re-embarked and sailed away on September 3.

At the moment of departure the Order had left 600 men capable of bearing arms, but the losses of the Ottomans had been yet more fearful. The most reliable estimate puts the number of the Turkish army at its height at some 40,000 men, of which but 15,000 returned to Constantinople. It was a most inglorious ending to the reign of Solyman the Magnificent.

Chapter III

THE CONSTITUTION OF THE ORDER OF ST. JOHN

Before proceeding to trace the history of the last two centuries of the Knights at Malta it will perhaps be advisable to examine the organization of an Order which was the greatest and most long-lived of all the medieval Orders of Chivalry. The siege of 1565 was its last great struggle with its mortal foe; after that there is but little left for the historian but to trace its gradual decadence and fall. And, as might be expected in a decadent society, though outwardly the constitution changed but little in the last two centuries, yet gradually the Statutes of the Order and the actual facts became more and more divergent.

There were three classes of members in the Hospitallers, who were primarily distinguished from each other by their birth, and who were allotted different functions in the Order. The Knights of Justice* were the highest class of the three and were the only Knights qualified for the Order's highest distinctions. Each langue had its own regulations for admitting members, and all alike exercised severe discrimination. Various kinds of evidence were necessary to prove the pure and noble descent of the candidate. The German was the strictest and most exacting of the langues, demanding proof of sixteen quarters of nobility and refusing to accept the natural sons of Kings into the ranks of its Knights. Italy was the most lenient, since

---

* So called because they were Knights "by right" of noble birth.

banking and trade were admitted as no stain on nobility, while most of the other langues insisted on military nobility only.

The chaplains, who formed the second class of the Order, were required to be of honest birth and born in wedlock of families that were neither slaves nor engaged in base or mechanical trades. The same regulations were in force for the third class — that of servants-at-arms, who served under the Knights both on land and sea. As the military character of the Order became less and less marked in the seventeenth and eighteenth centuries, these servants-at-arms became fewer and fewer, but in earlier days they were of considerable importance. The chaplains performed their duties at the Convent or on the galleys; the priests at the various commanderies throughout Europe were a class apart, known as Priests of Obedience, and never came to Malta, but resided permanently in their respective countries. A number of commanderies was allotted to the two inferior classes.

The Order, as we know, was an international one, and for purposes of administration was divided into sections or langues. In the sixteenth century there were eight of these divisions, which, in order of seniority, were Provençe, Auvergne, France, Italy, Aragon, England, Germany, and Castile. When Henry VIII suppressed the English langue in 1540, the Knights, with a reluctance to face the facts which was characteristic of a proud Order of Chivalry, kept up the fiction of its existence. In 1782, when the Elector of Bavaria secured the establishment of a Bavarian langue, it was united to the dormant langue of England and named the Anglo-Bavarian.

Each langue had its own quarters at the Convent known as the "Auberge," presided over by a "conventual bailiff," who in all matters was the head of the langue. Each conventual bailiff had an important office in the hierarchy of the Order which was permanently appurtenant to the headship of that langue. Thus the conventual bailiff of the langue of France was always the Grand Hospitaller in charge of the Hospital of the Order, while that of England was Turcopolier, or commander of the light cavalry — a survival from the Syrian days. The possessions of each langue in its native land were divided into grand priories and bailiwicks. Thus England, which meant the possessions throughout the British Isles, was divided into the Grand Priory of England at Clerkenwell, the Grand Priory of Ireland at Kilmainham, and the Bailiwick of the Eagle, which was situated near Lincoln and had originally belonged to the Templars. These Grand Priors and Bailiffs of each langue, as well as its conventual bailiff, were all Knights Grand Cross, and, as such, entitled to seats in the Chapter-General of the Order.

The supreme control of the Order was vested in the Chapter-General, consisting of all the Knights Grand Cross. Though these Chapters-General were often convened in the early history of the Order, their difficulty of assembly and their clumsy method of procedure made them less and less frequently summoned, as the

Grand Master had it in his power to convoke it when he pleased, though an interval of five years — later extended to ten — had been sanctioned by custom. In the seventeenth century the institution fell into utter disuse, and there was no meeting of the Chapter-General from 1631 to 1776, when its uselessness was finally demonstrated.

When the Chapter-General was not sitting the government of the Order was carried on by the Grand Master and the Councils, known as the Ordinary, Complete, Secret, and Criminal. The Ordinary Council consisted of the Grand Master, the conventual bailiffs, together with any Grand Cross residing at the Convent. This Council, as its name indicates, transacted the ordinary business of government, which mainly consisted of appointing to these offices and making those arrangements which were not definitely assigned to the Grand Master himself. The Secret and Criminal Councils, respectively, dealt with foreign affairs and offences against the Statutes, while the Complete, consisting of the Ordinary Council with the addition of two Knights from each langue of more than five years' residence at the Convent, dealt with appeals from the other Councils. In the later days of the Order the pernicious practice of appealing to the Pope destroyed all semblance of authority in this Council.

The election of the Grand Master was an exceedingly complicated affair, the intention being to prevent intrigue. Each langue solemnly elected three Knights to represent it, and this body of twenty-four chose a triumvirate, which consisted of a Knight, a chaplain, and a servant-at-arms. These three co-opted a fourth, and the four a fifth, and so on, till the number of sixteen was reached, and this body of sixteen elected the Grand Master. Every stage of the proceedings was hedged about with meticulous precautions to prevent intrigue and corruption, and it was a thoroughly typical medieval attempt to secure an honest election.

The framers of the Order's Statutes had taken the precaution of limiting the authority of the Grand Master by a minute enumeration of all his rights. But, as the Order developed into a purely military body, even officially his powers became greater. No subject for discussion could be introduced at the Councils except by himself; he had a double vote, and, in case of an equal division, a casting vote also; he had the right of nomination to many administrative posts besides all those of his own household, and in each priory there was a commandery in his own gift whose revenues went to himself. But even such wide powers were less than the reality. While the Order was at Rhodes, and during the first half-century at Malta, it was obviously necessary that the Grand Master should possess the powers of a commander-in-chief. As a purely military body, surrounded by powerful foes, the Order was in the position of an army encamped in enemy territory. Further, the absolute possession of Rhodes, and later of Malta, tended to give the Grand Masters the rank of independent Sovereigns, and the outside world regarded them as territorial potentates rather than as heads of an Order of aristocratic Knights.

But when the Order's existence was no longer threatened the Grand Master's position was assailed from many sides. No one, while reading the history of the Knights, can fail to be impressed by the numerous disturbances among them during the last 200 years of the Order. Drawn from the highest ranks of the nobility, young, rich, and with very little to occupy their time (except when on their "caravans"), the Knights were perpetually quarreling among themselves or defying the constituted authorities of the Order.

Charles V had insisted on keeping in his own hands the nomination of the bishopric of Malta, and the custom grew up that the Bishop of Malta and the Prior of St. John — the two most important ecclesiastics in the Order — should be chosen from the chaplains who were natives of the island. This was intended as a compensation for an injury which had been inflicted on the Maltese. To prevent the Grand Mastership falling into the hands of a native, the Maltese members of the Order were unable to vote at the election. The Bishop was often engaged in quarrels with the Grand Master, and the disputes were generally carried to the Pope, who, as the Head of Christendom, was regarded as having supremacy over all Religious Orders. But the Pope himself often encroached upon the rights of the Order, not only by sending nuncios to Malta with large and undefined powers, but by arrogating to himself the patronage of the langue of Italy when he wished to bestow gifts upon his relatives and friends. This led to bitter resentment among the Italian Knights, who saw all the lucrative posts of their langue given away to strangers. The introduction of the Inquisition in 1574 and the Jesuits in 1592, brought additional disputes about the chief authority in the island, and these different ecclesiastical personages had no hesitation in interfering in matters which should have been entirely beyond their province. Many a Grand Master of the seventeenth and eighteenth centuries had his time occupied in efforts to assert his authority.

The Grand Mastership was also weakened by the practice of electing very old men to the post, as the short tenure of the office and the feebleness of its holder meant a lax control over the turbulent Knights. This practice became very common in the last two centuries of the Order's existence. But many of the Grand Masters, though over seventy at the time of election, disappointed expectation by living till eighty or even ninety.

We possess detailed accounts of the financial system of the Order in the work of two Knights, Boisgelin and Boisredon de Ransijat, accounts which agree almost entirely.

The average revenue of the Order before the French Revolution was £136,000 per annum — i.e., the revenue which definitely reached Malta. It is to be remembered that this sum only represented the residue which was sent to the *chef-lieu.* The Knights possessed over 600 estates throughout Europe, each of which, besides sending contributions to Malta, maintained several members of the Order, gave a liberal income to its commander, and contributed towards the revenues of the Grand Priory in which it was situated. The chief items of the above sum were:

I. RESPONSIONS.

A proportion of the net income of each commandery fixed by the Chapter-General and liable to increase in case of need — £547,520 per annum.

2. MORTUARY AND VACANCY.

On the death of a commander all the net revenues from the day of his death to the following May I went to the Treasury: this was the MORTUARY; the whole revenue of the succeeding year was also sent to Malta: this was called the VACANCY — £521,470 per annum.

3. PASSAGES.

These were sums paid for admission into the Order, and were especially heavy for those who wished to enter the Order at an age earlier than that laid down in the Statutes — £520,324 per annum.

4. SPOILS.

These were the effects of deceased Knights, who were only allowed to dispose of one-fifth of their property by will, the remainder going to the Treasury — £524,755.

These made up about five-sixths of the total revenue, the remainder being small sums accruing from various sources, such as the proceeds from the timber of the commanderies (which went entirely to the Council), rents from buildings in Malta, and so forth.

At the height of their prosperity the Knights derived a very considerable revenue from their galleys, and just as Algiers, Tunis, or Tripoli throve on piracy, even so the wealth of the East contributed largely to the splendor of Malta. But during the seventeenth century various Christian Powers, such as Venice or France, insisted on restricting the Knights' claims to unlimited seizure of infidel vessels and infidel property on board ship. As early as 1582 the Pope had forbidden the Order to seize in a Christian harbor Turkish ships or Turkish property on Christian ships, and, despite the strenuous opposition of the Knights, enforced his commands.

The expenditure of the Order was, on the whole, within the limits of its revenue. The chief charge upon the expenditure was the fighting forces — the fleet and the garrisons — which together absorbed about half the revenue. Of the other items, the most important were the Hospital, the Churches of the Order, and the support of its officers both at the Convent and in the various European countries. The Knights were never seriously threatened financially till the French Revolution wiped out half their revenues at one fell swoop. Emergencies were always successfully met by an appeal to the self-denial of the members of the Order and the generosity of Europe.

The control of the revenues was in the hands of the Chambre de Commun Trésor, which consisted of eight officials, the most important of whom were the President, who was always the Grand Commander (the conventual bailiff of Provençe, the senior langue of the Order), and the Secretary through whose hands all the revenues passed. In each langue certain specified towns were used as receiving Treasuries, under the control of receivers who paid the money direct to the Central Treasury; these towns numbered twenty-nine in all. These receivers obtained the revenues from each estate or commandery within their district. At first the Order had possessed one common chest, but with the growth of its possessions each Grand Prior was put in control of his Priory's revenues; this proving unsatisfactory, from the difficulty of exercising control over these powerful Knights, the finances of each estate were administered by the commanders themselves, who dealt directly with the receivers in their area. They paid their quota or "responsions" biennially, and were subject to inspection from their Grand Priors; commanderies were rewards to aged Knights, and good administration brought promotion to richer estates.

The Criminal Council, which consisted of the Grand Master, the Bishop of Malta, the Prior of St. John, the conventual bailiffs, and any Grand Crosses present at the Convent, dealt with offences against the estates of the Order. The accused were brought in, the evidence taken, and the verdict declared. All evidence was verbal and no written testimony was accepted; each Knight, unless he could show good reason to the contrary, had to plead in person. Any English or German Knights, who knew only their own tongue and so had difficulty in being understood, were allowed advocates. The Order, by its Statutes, discouraged litigation to the utmost, desiring to promote concord and harmony among its members, and for that reason all legal procedure was made as simple and as summary as possible.

In such an exclusive and aristocratic Order there was naturally much jealousy of the power of its head. Facts gave the Grand Master a very strong position, but technically he was only *primus inter pares.* To make sure the Knights were not oppressed, they were always at liberty to disregard the Grand Master's or any superior's command and to appeal to a Court of Égard to prove that the given command was a violation of the Order's Statutes. The Court of Égard consisted of nine members, each langue choosing one from its own ranks, and the Grand Master appointing the President. Either disputant could object to any member of the Court, whereupon that member's langue chose a substitute. After hearing the evidence, which was entirely oral, the Court discussed the case behind closed doors and came to a decision. The litigants were called back, and if they agreed to accept the verdict the Court's decision was announced and was deemed final; if they refused to accept it, an appeal lay to another Court, called the Renfort of the Égard, which was constituted by each langue electing another member, thus doubling the original number. The same procedure was carried out as in the first Court, and if the litigants expressed themselves still dissatisfied, a new Court was summoned, called the Renfort of the Renfort, which was formed by the election from each langue of another member, thus making twenty-five with the President. If their decision was not accepted a final Court of Appeal, called the Bailiffs' Égard, was formed by the addition of the conventual bailiffs, or, if absent, their lieutenants, and their decision was final. This admirable Court of Equity existed almost unaltered right down to 1798.

The Hospital was a characteristic institution of the Order, and deserves some mention. Originally the chief scene of their activities, the Hospital was never forgotten by the Knights. Their first duty, wherever they went, was always to build a Hospital to tend the sick, and to the end every Knight at the Convent, in theory at least, went to take his turn in attending at the Hospital for one day in the week. The site of the Hospital, on the southeast side of Valetta, has been condemned by science as unhealthy, and it is very easy with modern knowledge to find many faults in its organization. Howard, in his "Lazarettos in Europe," in 1786, gave a vivid description of its condition and exposed its defects. At that time, however, the Hospital was sharing the general decadence of the Order, and discipline had become very lax. But, even so, the Hospital was far superior to most other hospitals in Europe and still kept much of that distinction it had acquired in the great days of the Order. We must remember that hospital organization is a very recent science, and it would be unfair to accuse the Knights of neglecting what had not yet been discovered. Their Hospital was one of the most famous in Europe, and was used by many from Sicily and Southern Italy as well as by the natives of Malta. It was open to all who wished to use it, and the attendance of patients from a distance proved that it supplied a need. The hospital, which had generally over 400 invalids, was maintained at great cost to the Order, and the regulations were drawn up with great care, though they reveal an amazing ignorance of some fundamental laws of health. Patients, for instance, who were members of the Order received meals twice as large as other patients.

Chapter IV

THE DECLINE, 1565–1789

The history of the Order of St. John after the siege of Malta in 1565 is a sad story of gradual and inevitable decay. The magnificent heroism of the Knights at the siege raised their fame throughout Europe to the highest pitch, and the siege was rightly regarded as one of the first decisive checks received by the Ottoman conquerors.

It is easy to imagine the anxious expectation of Europe in that summer of 1565, when the heretic Queen of England ordered prayers to be offered in the diocese of Salisbury for the safety of the Knights of St. John.

The Battle of Lepanto, six years later, despite its lack of immediate results, dissolved the spell which the invincibility of the Ottoman fleet had woven, and in the seventeenth century the Turkish Empire showed plainly that it had passed its meridian. Now that they were in a weakened condition, the Ottomans, though never fully regarded as a European Power, were more acceptable to the Christian States, most of whom followed the example of Francis I and concluded commercial agreements and treaties with the Porte. The Turk was no longer regarded as a being beyond human intercourse, and the Levant trade was too valuable to be ignored by France, England, or the Italian republics.

The Knights of Malta, with their attitude of truceless war against the infidel, were thus becoming more and more of an anachronism as time went on. They never concluded peace with the Sultan, and always regarded the possessions of the infidel as fair and lawful booty. It was obviously impossible for the Christian States trafficking in Turkish waters to allow such a theory to go unchallenged, and we therefore find the Order quarreling with the Pope, Venice, England, and France, as to their rights of seizure of Turkish goods in Christian vessels or of Turkish vessels in Christian harbors. In 1582 this led to a dispute with Gregory XIII, and in 1666 with Louis XIV, and the Knights were forced to confine their attentions to Turkish vessels trading between Turkish ports. England was destined later to incur similar trouble with neutrals for a similar theory of international law.

Had the Knights wished, their unending warfare against the Mohammedan would have found a suitable enemy in the Barbary Corsairs, who were a plague to Europe right to the year 1816; but though we find many a struggle between Knight and Corsair in the seventeenth century, the sloth and decadence that were mastering the Order made it gradually neglect its duty in that direction. Whatever energies they had were more profitably spent in the Levant; for the Knights, in their seafaring expeditions, became little more than Corsairs themselves. When it was necessary, as at the twenty-five years' siege of Candia (1644–1669), the Knights displayed once more that magnificent heroism that had made their name ring throughout the world. We find through the seventeenth century many a display of bravery, but they became more and more infrequent, till, in the eighteenth century, the Order's squadron was used for little else but show voyages to different Mediterranean ports. It was becoming too great a task even to raid Turkish merchantmen.

After the siege it was determined to move the *chef-lieu* of the Order from Il Borgo to Mount Sceberras, and on March 28, 1566, the building of Valetta was commenced. It was originally intended to bring the hill down to a certain level and on the plateau thus constructed to build the city. The fear of another Turkish invasion, however, did not allow of the completion of this plan, with the result that Valetta consists of a long, narrow plateau with slopes descending to Marso Muscetto on one side and the Grand Harbor on the other. The difficulty of moving about in this hilly town is commemorated in Byron's lines:

Adieu, ye joys of La Valette,
Adieu, sirocco, sun, and sweat,
Adieu, ye cursed streets of stairs,
How surely he who mounts you swears.

Each Grand Master strove to enlarge and strengthen the town's fortifications, with the result that, in the eighteenth century, Valetta was recognized as one of the greatest fortresses in the world. The building and upkeep of these fortifications proved a great drain upon the resources of the Order, and served but little purpose, except that of ministering to the vanity of successive Grand Masters, who desired to leave behind them memorials of themselves by bestowing their name upon a new fort or outwork. The continual increase of security and strength did not serve to improve the daring of the Knights, but rather helped to engender a condition of sloth that was destined to prove fatal.

This period is marked by constant tumults among the members of the Order and by acts of defiance against the Grand Masters. Even in the days of its glory there had been much jealousy and friction between the different nationalities composing the Order. The three French langues of Provençe, Auvergne, and France, by acting together, exercised a preponderant influence; they contributed half the revenues of the Order, and were generally able to secure their object against the opposition of the remaining Knights. The constant wars between Spain and France in the sixteenth and seventeenth centuries led to constant troubles at Malta, and the Grand Masters throughout this period had great and increasing difficulty in preserving the Order's neutrality. Many Knights broke their Oath of Obedience by enlisting in the French and Spanish armies. When this was discovered, the offended King would make out that the Order had taken sides and would threaten it with his vengeance. As the Order possessed many estates in both kingdoms, the Grand Masters were in constant fear that these would be encroached upon if an excuse could be found to justify such an action. But Spain, while it possessed the kingdom of the Two Sicilies, possessed an even surer method of punishing the Order. Malta, despite all the care lavished upon it, has never been able to produce sufficient corn for its population, and for this reason imported food regularly from Sicily, where the Order had built granaries for storing the corn while awaiting transshipment. As soon as the Knights offended the King of Spain Malta was plunged into scarcity, and the unhappy natives had often to suffer heavily because the Grand Master was a Frenchman.

Another result of the wars of France and Spain was the frequent internal quarrels at Malta. As the feelings of the two nations towards each other were often embittered, it is not surprising to find that French and Spanish Knights would come to open blows in the streets of Valetta. The unhealthy life of those young and idle aristocrats was conducive to turbulence, and the Grand Masters often adopted the policy of sending them to sea as soon as trouble was foreseen. The French were generally in the preponderance, as we can see from the great number of French Grand Masters; and the increasing greatness of the French monarchy in the seventeenth century was reflected at Malta.

The position of the Maltese became worse and worse as the Order declined. The natives, who had enjoyed a considerable measure of local autonomy under Spanish rule, had been very reluctant to submit to the Knights, and had protested to Charles V against their surrender to the Order, as a violation of the promise given in 1428 by Alphonse of Sicily that Malta would never be separated from the Sicilian Crown. They knew that the Order would conduct itself in Malta as a garrison in a fortress, and that this would mean strict military control over the inhabitants. It was also probable that the Turks would again besiege the Knights, as they had done at Rhodes in 1480 and 1522, and the Maltese were strongly averse to being drawn into such danger.

During the residence of the Knights the native population of Valetta was considerably modified. Some of the Rhodians who had, in 1523, accompanied the Knights, came with them to Malta; mercenaries who fought for the Order sometimes stayed on in the island, and many in this new population were illegitimate children of the Knights. For, though the vow of chastity was insisted on to the end as a condition of entrance into the Order, in practice, by the eighteenth century, it had become entirely ineffective.

At first the Knights made but slight inroads on the privileges of the natives, curtailing them only so far as was necessary for their military security, and imposing but few taxes upon them. As the island grew rich with the wealth brought in by the raids of the Knights, the condition of the Maltese also improved, and while the Order flourished it was not an excessive burden to the natives. But when the Knights started upon their decline the condition of the islanders deteriorated. They had always suffered from the occasional scarcity due to the ill-humor of the Spanish King or the natural failure of the Sicilian harvest. But now the taxes became heavier and heavier, and the free services of the Maltese, either as laborers in the constant fortifying of Valetta, or as soldiers in the garrison, or as sailors in the fleet, were more and more rigorously exacted. Many natives lost their lives while fighting with the Order, and from the generous behavior of Grand Masters to the native women and children, which we find mentioned in chronicles, we can see there was occasionally acute distress in the island.

In its degeneracy the Order treated the Maltese with boundless contempt, as might be expected from spoiled members of the great

European aristocracies towards petty islanders. One of the most intolerable forms of the arrogance of the Knights during their last years at Malta was their disgusting behavior towards the womenfolk of the natives; complaint was dangerous and futile. When the British captured the island in October, 1800, the mere proposal to restore the Order raised such a storm of protest from the Maltese as to prove conclusively to all how hated had been the domination of the Knights.

The splendor of the Knights at the height of their greatness can be judged from the many magnificent buildings they constructed in the island. The Church of St. John in particular received such careful and lavish attention that it became one of the most splendid churches in Christendom, being especially famous for its wonderful mosaic floor. The "auberges" of the various langues were also built in the most magnificent manner, and the palace of the Grand Master at Valetta was a sumptuous building worthy of a king.

The decline of the Order brought with it a diminution of respect from the nations of Europe, and we read of constant and increasing interference from outside in the affairs of the Order. The greatest offender was the Pope, who had always enjoyed a nominal headship over the Order, and who had been kept at a distance with difficulty even while the Knights had been at Rhodes. The creation of a bishopric at Malta, the introduction of the Inquisition, and then of the Jesuits, had led to constant quarrels between the Knights and the ecclesiastics, and from these had arisen the evil practice of appeals to the Curia. In the seventeenth century the Popes regarded the valuable patronage of the langue of Italy as in their gift, and the Grand Masters were powerless to protect their defrauded Knights. The depths of the Order's humiliation were shown by the demand of Pope Urban XIII, in 1642, that the Order's galleys should help him fight the League of Italian Princes which had been formed to resist his invasion of Parma. Lascaris, the Grand Master, was unable to refuse, and for the first time the famous red galleys were seen arrayed against Christian neighbors.

The operations of the Knights in the seventeenth century were mainly carried out in alliance with the Venetians, who were the one Power who continued to resist the Turk at sea. They were still lords of the great island of Crete, which lay athwart the trade routes of the Levant, and only by its conquest would the Ottoman control of the Eastern Mediterranean be complete. In 1645 Ibrahim I declared war on Venice and besieged Candia; but the attack was so remiss that success seemed impossible. The Knights of Malta threw themselves into the struggle on the side of the Venetians, feeling bound in honor to do so, as the refuge of Maltese galleys in Venetian harbors was the Turkish pretext for war. In 1656 Mocenigo, the Venetian Admiral, with the aid of the Knights, won a brilliant victory off the Dardanelles, capturing Lemnos and Tenedos. This imminent peril brought Mohammed Kiuprili to power as Grand Vizier, and the war was thenceforward conducted with great energy by the Turks. Year after year volunteers flocked to Candia to save the last Christian outpost in the Levant, but it was all fruitless, and in 1669 the island, with the exception of three ports, was surrendered to the Turks — their last important conquest in Europe, and the final term of their advance.

The seventeenth century saw the gradual displacement of galleys in favor of sailing ships. The long voyages across the Atlantic and to the East had given great impetus to the development of the sailing vessel; its increasing use, and the entrance of England and Holland into the Mediterranean, had shown the Powers of that sea its superiority over the galley; finally, slaves were becoming more difficult to obtain in sufficient quantities, while criminals had never been a satisfactory source of supply. The Knights were slow in changing the oar for the sail, and to the end kept a small squadron of galleys as well as men-of-war. When Napoleon captured the island, in 1798, he found there two men-of-war, one frigate, and four galleys.

The pride and the renown of the Order had always demanded a salute from the warships of other nations, and even the mighty Louis XIV yielded this privilege to the little squadron. There is extant an interesting correspondence between Charles II and the Grand Master, Nicholas Cottoner, on the subject of salutes. A squadron of the British Fleet, under Admiral Sir John Narborough, had refused to salute Valetta unless assured of a response from the guns of the fortress — a mark of respect that the Order was unwilling to pay to the British flag. The Grand Master had also ventured to doubt Narborough's rank as Admiral, but the affair was amicably settled to the satisfaction of all.

Though the decline of the Order was obvious to Europe throughout the eighteenth century, and the value of such a fortress as Malta to a Mediterranean Power apparent to all, yet there is little definite proof of any desire to wrest the island from the Knights. Of all the nations round the Mediterranean, France alone could be said not to be in a state of decay; Venice, Genoa, and Turkey were becoming more and more feeble at sea, and there was little fear of an attack on Malta from any of them; and though Spain paid great attention to her fleet in the second part of the eighteenth century, there was little reason to fear her aggression. Britain was acquiring greater and greater interests in the Mediterranean, but most of her attentions were directed to Spain and France. While the Knights kept their neutrality, however decadent and feeble they might be, there was little fear of their being disturbed. Europe still respected the relics of a glorious past of six centuries of unceasing warfare against the Moslem; but the moment that past with its survivals became itself anathema the Knights and their organization would collapse at once. The French Revolution meant death to the Knights of the Order of St. John as well as to other bodies of aristocrats.

Chapter V

THE FALL, 1789–1798

A wealthy Order of Knights drawn exclusively from the ranks of the nobility was sure to attract the attention of the French revolutionaries. Its international character was a cause of offence to the strong French nationalism engendered during the Revolution, while its traces of monastic organization helped to identify the Knights with the Church.

When Necker, in the financial distress of the autumn of 1789, appealed for a voluntary contribution from all landowners, the Order gave him a third of the revenue of its French commanderies, and later it pledged its credit for 500,000 francs to the destitute Louis XVI, to help him in the flight that ended so disastrously at Varennes. This last act put it in definite opposition to the Revolution.

The Constituent Assembly declared the Order of St. John to be a foreign Power possessing property in France, and, as such, liable to all taxes to be levied on natives, and immediately afterwards a decree was passed declaring that any Frenchman belonging to an Order of Knighthood which demanded proofs of nobility from entrants could not be considered a French citizen. This was followed by the main attack on September 19, 1792, when all the property in France was declared confiscate and annexed to the French national domains. There was some mention of indemnification to the despoiled Knights, but as the necessary condition to a pension was residence in France — a dangerous course for a noble in 1793 and 1794 — the scheme came to naught. The decree of

September, 1792, was the death-blow to the Order, and its extinction was simply a matter of time. The course of the war and the constant French successes made their position even more perilous. Half the revenues had gone with the confiscation in France; but this was not all, for Bonaparte's Italian campaigns meant the loss of the Order's estates in Northern Italy, and the conquests of the French on the Rhine diminished the German possessions. With decreasing resources and dwindling numbers, the fortress of Malta could not long hold out if attacked, and the position of the Order was becoming desperate. De Rohan, the Grand Master, temporized and refused to declare war on France, but he seems to have helped the Spanish and English fleets by allowing them to recruit at Malta, a privilege hitherto granted very sparingly by the Knights. But whatever the Grand Master's policy, no words or pretences could disguise the fact that the French Republic by its confiscation had assaulted the Order. It was only too probable that France would seize the first opportunity of attacking the Order in its own home and by this means increasing its power in the Mediterranean.

One gleam of light came to cheer the gloom at Malta. The third dismemberment of Poland had brought the Polish Priory into the hands of the Tsar Paul I. Among other eccentricities of that monarch was a passionate admiration for chivalry, which he displayed by changing the Polish into a Russian Priory, increasing its revenues to 300,000 florins, and incorporating it in the Anglo-Bavarian langue; he also assumed the title of "Protector of the Order of Malta."

In 1797, at Ancona, Napoleon had intercepted a message from the Tsar to the Grand Master containing this news. Plans for the capture of Malta took shape in Bonaparte's mind, and he sent a cousin of the French consul at Malta, Poussièlgue by name, to spy out the condition of the island, at the same time ordering Admiral Brueys, on his journey from Corfu to Toulon, to examine the situation of Malta.

When the expedition to Egypt was decided upon, the capture of Malta formed part of the instructions to Napoleon.

Bonaparte, relying on the demoralization of the island, intended the capture to be a swift piece of work, and Poussièlgue had helped him by winning over some natives and French Knights to his side. The Grand Master, Von Hompesch, seems to have been utterly unnerved by the bewildering problems before him, and the cowardice and irresolution he displayed were a disgrace to the traditions of the Order. Speed was essential to the French army, as discovery by Nelson would be fatal to Bonaparte's plans, but had Von Hompesch been an utter traitor the capitulation could not have been more sudden and disgraceful and beneficial to the enemy.

On June 6 the vanguard of the French appeared off the island, and on the 9th it was joined by the main fleet, the whole now numbering about 450 sail, of which 14 were ships of the line and 30 were frigates; the Grand

Master had about 300 Knights and 6,000 men, chiefly Maltese, under arms. Had this garrison been resolute and united, the fortifications of Valetta could have held the French for a considerable time. But the natives were divided, many regarding the French, despite their doubtful career of the last few years, as liberators from a detestable tyranny. Two-thirds of the Knights were French, and many of them had become infected with republican principles, though the French langues also contained the fiercest opponents to the invaders.

Bonaparte sent for permission for his fleet to enter the harbor for water and for his soldiers to land — a request which was tantamount to a demand for surrender. Von Hompesch sent back a conciliatory letter, saying that treaty obligations forbade the entrance of more than four vessels at a time. Napoleon thereupon threw off the mask, and during the night landed troops at seven different parts of the island. A slight resistance was encountered from a few detached forts, but by the evening of the 10th

Valetta was closely invested. The mob was encouraged by hired emissaries to attack as traitors the Knights, who were really the most bitter enemies of the invaders. While Napoleon's agents were busy throughout the town, Von Hompesch sat motionless in his palace, and no subordinate commander would take the responsibility of firing on the besiegers. Finally, a party of citizens interviewed Von Hompesch and threatened to surrender the town if he refused to capitulate.

At this point a mutiny broke out in the garrison, and the Grand Master and his Council, seeing the hopelessness of the situation, sent for an armistice preliminary to surrender. The armistice was concluded on the 11th, and on the 12th Napoleon entered Valetta, full of amazement at the might of the fortress he had so easily captured. On the 12th the capitulation was drawn up, of which the main clauses were:

1. The Knights surrendered Malta and its sovereignty to the French army.

2. The French Republic would try to secure to the Grand Master an equivalent principality and would meanwhile pay him an annual pension of 300,000 livres.

3. The French would use their influence with the different Powers assembled at Rastadt to allow the Knights who were their subjects to control the property of their respective langues.

4. French Knights were allowed to return to France.

5. French Knights in Malta were to receive a pension from the French Government of 700 livres per annum; if over sixty years old, 1,000 livres.

Such was the end of the Order at Malta. Napoleon treated the Knights and the Grand Master with extreme harshness. Most of them were required to leave within three days, and some even within twenty-four hours.

On June 18, Von Hompesch, taking with him the three most venerable relics of the Order

— all that the conqueror allowed him from the treasures at Valetta — left for Trieste, whence he withdrew to Montpellier, dying there in obscurity in 1805. Most of the homeless Knights proceeded to Russia, where, on October 27, 1798, Paul I was elected Grand Master, though Von Hompesch still held the post.

But on the Tsar's death in 1801 the Order lost the one man who might have been powerful enough to bring about a restoration, and the survival of some scattered relics could not conceal the fact that vanished forever was the Order of the Hospital of St. John of Jerusalem.

Appendix I

SOVEREIGNTY OF THE ORDER

There can be no doubt whatever that, after 1530, the Order was no longer independent and sovereign, and that L'Isle Adam, despite all his efforts, had become a feudatory, though the service demanded was very slight. The Act of Donation of Malta put them definitely into the position of feudal vassals of Charles V as King of the two Sicilies. This is plain to everyone who examines the Charter itself (Vertot, III, p. 494, or Codice Diplomatico, II, p. 194). The tenure on which the Knights held the island from the King of the Sicilies may be classed as a form of serjeanty — the annual payment of a falcon being the only feudal service demanded. There were other conditions in the Charter concerning the Bishop of Malta and the Grand Admiral of the Order, but they were not strictly feudal. The chroniclers of the Order were naturally reluctant to admit this, and as the feudal tie was very weak, they glossed it over. But the Sovereign of the island, strictly speaking, was the King of the two Sicilies, and the Knights were never more than tenants. When the Order had been expelled by Napoleon we can see this universally admitted. While the fate of the island was in doubt — that is, before the preliminary peace between England and France in 1801 — both natives and English regarded the King of Naples as lord of the island (Hardman, III, 142. Foreign Office Records, Sicily, 11). When the Maltese wanted to be put under the protection of England, either temporarily or, later, permanently (Hardman, 185, 193, 204), they applied to the King of the Sicilies, as their lawful Sovereign, to grant their request. Events soon made Malta a question of great importance in the relations between France and England, and the renewal of war, in 1803, left Great Britain in *de facto* possession of the island, until the treaty of May 30, 1814, gave England full right and sovereignty over Malta.

Appendix II

CONNECTION BETWEEN KNIGHTS OF MALTA AND THE MODERN ORDER OF ST. JOHN

During the Napoleonic wars the surviving Knights were too scattered and too helpless to be able to improve their condition. But from 1815 onwards we find various attempts of the Order to obtain from Europe another *chef-lieu*, and representatives of the Knights at the Congress of Vienna (1815) and at the Congress of

Verona (1822) tried in vain to persuade the Allies to grant them an island. The French Knights were by far the largest and most powerful section of the Order, and in 1814 they had established a capitular commission in which they vested plenary powers to treat on their behalf. During the various negotiations for a *chef-lieu* the question of reviving the English langue was started, and the French Commission entered into communication with the Rev. Sir Robert Peat, Chaplain to King George IV, and other distinguished Englishmen. The outcome was the reconstitution of the English langue on January 24, 1831, with Sir Robert Peat as Grand Prior.

The English branch of the Order of St. John has devoted itself for the last ninety years to the succor of the sick and wounded, setting up cottage and convalescent hospitals, aiding the sick in other hospitals, and establishing ambulance litters in dangerous industrial centers, such as coal-mines and railway-stations, which at last developed into the St. John Ambulance

Association, which rendered such magnificent service during the Great War. The German branch of the Order was the first to start ambulance work in the field in the Seven Weeks' War of 1866, work which was continued in the Franco-Prussian War of 1870. Since that date the mitigation of the sufferings of war has been a conspicuous part of the work of the Order of St. John, and nowhere has the Order's magnificent spirit of international comradeship been more fully displayed.

Books Consulted

PRIMARY AUTHORITIES

Statuta Ordinis Domus Hospitalis Hierusalem. Edited by Fr. Didacus Rodriguez. Rome. 1556.

Statuti della religione de Cavalieri Gierosolimitani. Florence. 1567.

Statuta Hospitalis Hierusalem. Rome. 1588.

Collection of Statutes in Volume IV of Vertot's Histoire de Chevaliers de Malte. Paris. 1726.

[As there was no Chapter-General between 1631 and 1776, all the above collections are practically complete, Vertot's containing little more than the others.]

Codice Diplomatico del sacro militare ordine Gierosolimitano oggi di Malta. Fr. Sebastiano Pauli. Lucca. 1737.

Letters and Papers, Foreign and Domestic. 1523–1547.

Calendar of State Papers. (Foreign.) 1547–1585.

Calendar of State Papers. (Venetian.)

Calendar of State Papers. (Spanish.)

Les Archives de S. Jean de Jerusalem à Malte. Delaville Le Roulx. Paris. 1883.

Report of Philip de Thame. Grand Prior of England. 1338. Camden Society. Volume LXV. 1857.

Armoury of the Knights of St. John of Jerusalem at Malta. Edited by G.F. Laking. London. 1903.

Carta y verdadera relacion escrita por il eminentissimo Señor Gran Maestre al Commendador Fr. Don Joseph Vidal. 1669.

E Tanner. Notitia Monastica. Ed. James Nasmith. Cambridge. 1787.

Malte. Par un Voyageur français. Anonymous. 1791.

Le Monete e Medaglie del S. Ordine Gierosolimitano. C. Taggiasco. Camerino. 1883.

Relation du Voyage et Description exacte de Malte. Paris. 1779.

Malta illustrata. Giovanni Abela. Malta. 1772–1780. 2 Volumes.

Liste de Chevaliers des Langues de Provençe, Auvergne et France. Malta. 1772.

SECONDARY AUTHORITIES

GIACOMO BOSIO: Dell' Istoria della sacra religione et ill'ma Militia di San Giovanni Gierosolimitano. Rome. 1594. 2 volumes.

ABBÉ DE VERTOT: Histoire des Chevaliers de Malte. Paris. 1726. 4 volumes.

CHEVALIER DE BOISGELIN: Malta Ancient and Modern. English edition. 2 volumes. 1804.

PRESCOTT: Life of Philip II. Volume II.

MAJOR-GENERAL PORTER: History of the Knights of Malta. Revised edition. I volume. London. 1883.

DE GOUSSANCOURT: Le Martyrologe des Chevaliers de S. Jean de Hierusalem. Paris. 1643.

ANONYMOUS: Memoire de' Gran Maestri del sacro militare ordine Gierosolimitano. Parma. 1780.

L. HÉRITTE: Essai sur l'Ordre des Hospitaliers de S. Jean de Jérusalem. Paris. 1912.

HARDMAN: History of Malta, 1798–1815. Edited by J. Holland Rose. London. 1909.

REV. W.K.R. BEDFORD: Malta and the Knights Hospitallers. London. 1894.

REV. W.K.R. BEDFORD: The Hospital at Malta. Edinburgh. 1882.

J. TAAFE: History of the Order of S. John. 4 volumes. London. 1852.

A.T. DRANE: History of the Order of St. John. London. 1881.

MIÈGE: Histoire de Malte. 3 volumes. Paris. 1846.

M.M. BALLOU: Story of Malta. Boston and New York. 1893.

REV. W.K.R. BEDFORD AND R. HOLBECHE: Order of the Hospital of St. John of Jerusalem. London. 1902.

ADMIRAL JURIEN DE LA GRAVIERE: (1) Les Chevaliers de Malte et la Marine de Philippe II. Paris. 1887. (2) Les Corsaires barbaresques et la Marine de Solyman le Grand. Paris. 1884. (3) Les Marins du XV'e et XVI'e siècles. Paris. 1879. (4) Les derniers Jours de la Marine à Rames. Paris. 1885.

COMMANDER E.H. CURREY: Sea Wolves of the Mediterranean. London. 1913.

SIR JULIAN CORBETT: England in the Mediterranean, 1603–1713. 2 volumes. London. 1904.

S. LANE-POOLE: Barbary Corsairs. (Stories of the Nations.) 1886.

E. DRIAULT: La Question d'Orient. Paris. 1898.

J.A.R. MARRIOT: The Eastern Question. Oxford. 1917.

G. VIULLIER: Le Tour du Monde. Malte et les Maltais.

P.J.O. DOUBLET: L'Invasion et l'Occupation de Malte. Paris. 1883.

C.T.E. DE TOULGOET: Les Responsabilités de la Capitulation de Malte en 1798. (Revue des Questions Historiques. 1900.)

DE LA JONQUIÈRE: L'Expedition d'Égypte. Paris. 1901.

NOTE ON THE AUTHORITIES

For the Statutes of the Order we possess the Italian edition of 1567, two Latin editions of 1556 and 1588, and the collection at the end of Vertot's fourth volume, which is later and more complete. The Codice Diplomatico of Fr. Pauli is the only collection of Charters to my knowledge which covers practically the whole history of the Order: the magnificent Cartulaire of Delaville Le Roulx only covers the Syrian period in the Knights' history. Many valuable hints can be found in the Calendars of State Papers issued by the Record Office, but they fail us at the beginning of the seventeenth century.

Of the various historians above mentioned, Bosio, for the period he covers, is by far the best and completest. Vertot only goes down to 1565: after the siege he treats the subject in a bare annalistic form. Boisgelin, who was a Knight himself and wrote his history after his expulsion from Malta, is valuable for his elaborate excursus on the financial system of the Order. All three — who are our completest authorities — wrote from the point of view of the Order, and consequently are very unreliable in some matters. The treatment that the Maltese received from the Order is very inadequately dealt with, and none of them can seriously estimate the Mediterranean background to the history of the Knights, and especially their relations with the Barbary pirates. General Porter, whose history is the only English one at all worthy of mention, possesses the same faults. Though his knowledge of the island is thorough, his ignorance of European history makes him neglect the importance of the external activities of the Knights, and he follows the Order's chroniclers too slavishly to claim authority as an independent investigator. Miège, who was a French Consul at Malta, is interesting as a bitter opponent of the Order and all its work; and he practically confines himself to the treatment of the Maltese at the hands of the Knights.

The best authority on sixteenth-century sea power in the Mediterranean is Admiral Jurien de la Gravière, while Commander Currey's book is very sound and interesting.

Lightning Source UK Ltd.
Milton Keynes UK
UKHW010355031221
394997UK00001B/36